Sally

Fit for five

Erarbeitet von
Jasmin Brune, Daniela Elsner,
Stefanie Gleixner-Weyrauch,
Simone Gutwerk,
Marion Lugauer, Sabine Schwarz

Illustriert von Wilfried Poll

Oldenbourg

Mit „Fit for five" kannst du überprüfen, was du schon alles im Englischunterricht gelernt hast. So kommst du gut vorbereitet in die 5. Klasse!

In jedem der 7 Kapitel kannst du zeigen,

 • dass du Wörter und kurze Texte verstehst,

 • dass du einige grundlegende Regeln im Englischen kennst,

 • dass du dich in wichtigen Situationen verständigen kannst.

Wähle ein Kapitel aus und bearbeite die Übungen. Die Wörterliste auf den Seiten 30–35 hilft dir dabei.

Kontrolliere mit den Lösungen ganz hinten im Heft, ob du alles richtig gemacht hast.

Danach gibt es noch kurze Tests zur Überprüfung.

Zum Schluss hakst du in einer Liste ab, was du schon kannst und was du noch üben musst.

1. Read the sentences. Write the correct numbers next to the pictures.

1. This is Tim. He is in class 4b.

2. This is Linda. She is in class 4b.

3. This is Susan. She is from England.

4. This is Tobi. He is from Germany.

5. This is John. He is ten years old.

6. This is Ann. She is ten years old.

2. He or she? Colour the words blue or red.

Mrs Miller

he

she

dad

Simon

Tina

Jenny

Mr Brown

John

Susan

3. What about you?

Hi. I'm _____ .

I'm from _____ .

I'm _____ years old.

I'm in class _____ .

I'm = I am

4. Tell more about yourself, your family and your friends.

_____

_____

_____

_____

 1. Odd one out!

June, February, Monday, December

brother, teacher, sister, mother

ten, eight, one, yellow

Big Ben, Australia, Germany, Great Britain

 **2.** Read and draw lines.

What's your name?   It's on the desk.

How old is Tim?   My name is Sally.

Where is Ann's pencil?   It's 8 o'clock.

When is your birthday?   He's 10 years old.

What time is it?   My birthday is in May.

3. Fill in: when, where, how, what.

_____ are you? – I'm fine, thanks.

_____ 's your name? – My name is Daniel.

_____ old are you? – I'm ten years old.

_____ are you from? – I'm from England.

_____ is your hobby? – My hobby is playing the guitar.

_____ is your birthday? – My birthday is in January.

> when = wann   how = wie
> where = wo   what = was

4. Put the words into the correct order. Write the sentences.

old is brother how your? How _____

time is what it? _____

you where live do? _____

is hobby what your? _____

to bed when do go you? _____ .

Im Englischen schreibst du die meisten Wörter klein.
Nur Satzanfänge, Eigennamen und einige besondere
Wörter (I, Wochentage, Monate) schreibst du groß.

5. Ben meets Sarah. Write the dialogue.

Grüße und stelle dich vor. Frage
das Mädchen nach dem Namen.

_____

_____

_____

Grüße zurück und
nenne deinen Namen.

_____

_____

Frage Sarah, wie es ihr geht.

_____

Antworte, dass es dir gut geht.
Frage Ben, woher er kommt.

_____

_____

Antworte, dass du
aus England kommst.

_____

Sage, dass du aus Deutschland
kommst. Verabschiede dich.

_____

_____

Verabschiede dich.

_____

Die Sätze von
Aufgabe 3 auf Seite 7
können dir helfen.

 **1.** Read the comic.

 **2.** What's wrong? Correct the sentences.

Sally is a cow. _____

Sally comes from Spain. _____

Her best friends are Kenny the kangaroo and Walter the horse.

_____

_____

Kenny and Walter come from Spain, too. _____

_____

Craig is Sally's friend. _____

He is nice. _____

He is a dog. _____

He loves to eat carrots, bananas and lollipops. _____

_____

3. Match the words.

elephant   bear   cat   goldfish   sheep   crocodile
horse   rabbit   budgie   hamster   duck   goose
snake   guinea pig   zebra

kangaroo

_____   _____

_____   (wild animals)   _____

_____   _____

_____   dog

_____   (pets)   _____

_____   _____

_____

cow

_____   _____

_____   (farm animals)   _____

_____

4. Sally has got some pictures on her mobile phone.

Circle the correct word: is or are, isn't or aren't.

Look, this is / are my house.

It isn't / aren't very big.

Here is / are my friends Kenny and Walter.

Kenny and Walter isn't / aren't kangaroos like me.

Kenny is / are a koala.

Walter is / are a wombat.

Craig isn't / aren't my friend.

He is / are a crocodile.

In der Einzahl verwendest du im Englischen is,
bei einer Verneinung isn't.
In der Mehrzahl verwendest du are, bei einer Verneinung aren't.

5. Write and talk about your pet or friend.

_____

_____

_____

_____

_____

… is my pet/my friend.
He's/She's a …
He's/She's … years old.
He's/She's from …
He's/She's big/small/
brown/nice …

1. Read and tick ✓ what Jack, Tom and Sarah can do.

Jack and Tom can play football. Sarah can play football, too.
Tom can't play the guitar, but he can sing.
Can Sarah ride a horse? Yes, she can. But Jack and Tom can't.
And what about Jack? Can he play the piano? No, he can't,
but he can play the guitar.

	play football	play the guitar	ride a horse	sing
Jack				
Tom				
Sarah				

2. Write down what the children can do and what they can't do.

Tom can play football, but he can't play hockey. _____

_____

_____

_____

_____

 **3.** Write a dialogue about Ann and Tom's hobbies.

Ann: Can you play the guitar? – Tom: Yes, I can.

Tom: Can you _____

_____

_____

_____

_____

Wenn du etwas kannst, dann sagst du im Englischen I can (swim) ☺.
Wenn du etwas nicht kannst, dann sagst du I can't (sing) ☹.

A perfect bed for me.

Stop, Sally! This is my home!

A perfect bed for Wombat and me!

1. Where do you live? Read the sentences. Find the correct pictures and draw lines.

I live in a castle.

I live in the ocean.

I live on a farm.

I live in an igloo.

I live in a tepee.

I live in the zoo.

2. Find 10 words in my house. Write.

_____

_____

_____

_____

_____

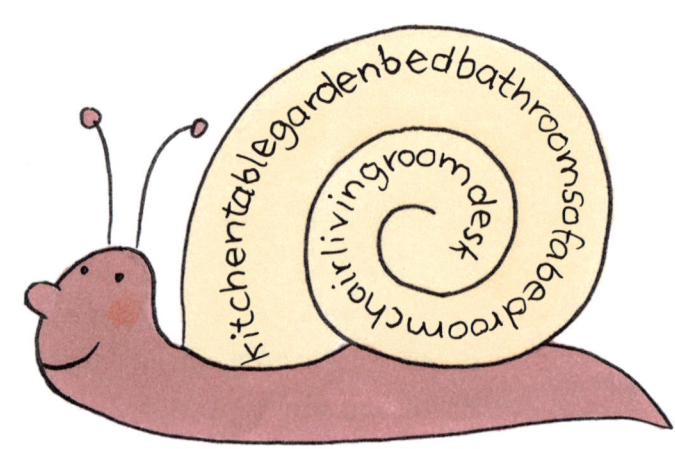

3. Come to my castle.

| kitchen | toilet | bathroom |
| garden | bedroom | living room |

Where is my lamp? The lamp is in the _____ .

Where is my toilet? The toilet is _____ .

Where is my horse? The _____ .

Where are my shoes? _____ .

Where is my sofa? _____ .

Where is my table? _____ .

Mit Präpositionen kannst du genauer beschreiben, wo sich etwas befindet.

| in | on | under | next to | behind | in front of |

 4. Look at the picture and write sentences.

| The | bike, skateboard, hamster schoolbag, books, dog, guitar, computer | is are | in, on, in front of, behind, under, next to | the | cupboard, bed sofa, shelves, chair, desk, door |

The bike is in the cupboard. _____

_____

_____

_____

_____

5. What about your room? Tell a friend.

My teddy bear is …

The books are …

My schoolbag is …

My T-shirts are …

The bed is …

My CD player is …

_____

_____

_____

_____

_____

Great!
A T-shirt for £2!

Mr Paper

Two for £1:

Half price:
10 pencils £3 £1.50
pencil case £12 £6
5 pens £3.60 £1.80
3 exercise books £2 £1

Special offer:
birthday card
only £1.99

1. What can you buy for £1?

_____

2. What can you buy for half price?

_____

3. What did Susan
buy at Mr Paper's?

_____	1,80
2 _____	3,98
6 _____	2,-
2 _____	1,-

 **4.** What does Sally buy at Mr Paper's?

Sally buys _____

_____

Bei den meisten englischen Nomen hängst du in der Mehrzahl ein **s** an:

 one pencil – five pencil**s**

! one sheep – six sheep, one fish – four fish, one mouse – three mice, **!**
one foot – two feet, one tooth – seven teeth

 **5.** Correct the mistakes.

Hello
~~Good night~~, Mr Paper.

I'd like
two bananas, please.

Thanks.
Good morning, Mr Paper.

Goodbye, Sally.
What would you like?

Here you swim.
That's £1, please.

Hello, Sally.

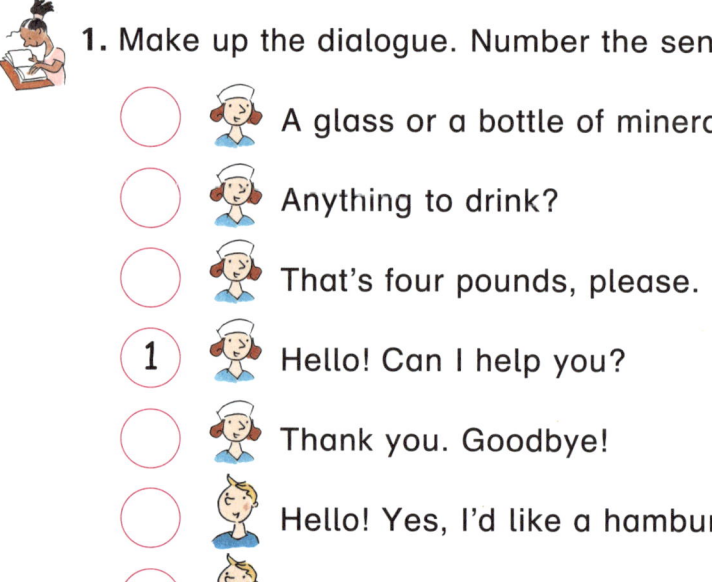 **1.** Make up the dialogue. Number the sentences in the correct order.

◯ A glass or a bottle of mineral water?

◯ Anything to drink?

◯ That's four pounds, please.

① Hello! Can I help you?

◯ Thank you. Goodbye!

◯ Hello! Yes, I'd like a hamburger.

◯ Four pounds. Here you are.

◯ I'd like some mineral water, please.

◯ A bottle of mineral water.

◯ Goodbye!

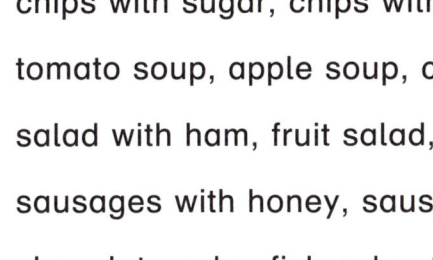

ham sandwiches, cheese sandwiches, lollipop sandwiches

chips with sugar, chips with ketchup, chips with salt

tomato soup, apple soup, carrot soup, cucumber soup

salad with ham, fruit salad, shoe salad, frog salad

sausages with honey, sausages with mashed potatoes

chocolate cake, fish cake, fruit cake

banana ice cream, lemon ice cream, kangaroo ice cream

2. Crazy menu! Write down what you like and what you don't like.

I like _____

_____

_____

_____

I don't like _____

_____

_____

_____

Wenn du etwas magst, dann sagst du im Englischen I like (salad) ☺.
Wenn du etwas nicht magst, dann sagst du I don't like (ketchup) ☹.

21

3. Sally wants something to eat and drink.
Make up the dialogue.

FOOD	DRINKS
pizza £1	orange juice £1
hamburger £1	coke £1
salad with ham £1,20	lemonade £1
fish and chips £1	tea £1
cheese sandwich £1	coffee £1
chicken sandwich £1,30	water £1

_____   _____

_____   _____

_____   _____

_____   _____

_____   _____

_____   _____

_____   _____

Die Sätze von Aufgabe 1
auf Seite 20 können dir helfen.
Denke auch an die Begrüßung
und Verabschiedung.

Test 1: Minnie's postcard

Read and write.

Hi Grandma,

London is great.
But it's very cold and rainy.
I like the double-decker buses!
Today we are going to a museum.
We want to be back home on Sunday.

Love, Minnie

Mrs Miller
5 Main Street
Manchester
A12 3BC

Where is Minnie?

_____

What's the weather like?

_____

What does Minnie like?

_____

Where is Minnie going today?

_____

When does Minnie want to be back home?

_____

Test 2: Funny animals

Read and colour.

The blue mouse is under the skateboard.
The red mouse is in the cake.
The cat with green legs is on the piano.
The orange guinea pig is next to the piano.
The horse with the purple head is in the lake.
The yellow horse is riding the bike.
The green dog is playing the guitar.

Test 3: Jumbled sentences

Put the words into the correct order.

a ruler and a book   I've got   in my schoolbag

_____.

on my desk   the pencil case   is

_____.

is   under my folder   the book

_____.

Test 4: What can you say?

Fill in the speech bubbles.

What's …	How much …
How old …	How …

_____? –

I'm fine, thanks!

_____? –

It's £5.

_____? –

My favourite fruit is banana.

Where are you from? –

_____

Can you play basketball? –

_____

_____? –

I'm 10 years old.

25

Hören: Ich kann Wörter und Sätze verstehen, wenn jemand langsam über mich, meine Familie oder meine Umwelt spricht.

	Kann ich	Muss ich noch üben
Ich verstehe, wenn jemand über seine Hobbys oder Freunde spricht und sagt:	○	○

I like playing basketball.
My best friend is Lisa.

Ich verstehe, wenn mich jemand nach meinem Namen, meinem Alter oder meinem Lieblingshaustier fragt:	○	○

What's your name?
How old are you?
What's your favourite pet?

Ich kann einfache Anweisungen befolgen, wie z.B.:	○	○

Stand up.
Pass me the butter, please.

Ich kann den Inhalt einer Geschichte verstehen, wenn sie mir erzählt oder vorgelesen wird und wenn ich die wichtigsten Wörter bereits kenne.	○	○

The clever tortoise
There's a lake in the African jungle ...

Sprechen: Ich kann Menschen, Tiere oder Dinge in einfachen Sätzen beschreiben und Informationen über mich selbst geben.

	Kann ich	Muss ich noch üben

Ich kann über mich selbst z. B. sagen, wie alt ich bin, wo ich wohne oder was meine Lieblingsfarbe ist:

I'm 10 years old.
I live in Berlin.
My favourite colour is red.

Ich kann Informationen über meine Geschwister, meine Eltern oder mein Haustier geben:

This is my cat.
Her name is Tibby.
Tibby is black.

Ich kann beschreiben, was ich auf einem Bild sehe:

There is a car.
The car is yellow.
It's in the street.

Ich kann kurze Geschichten, Reime oder ein Lied vortragen:

Head and shoulders,
knees and toes,
knees and toes …

27

Gespräche führen: Ich kann mich mit jemandem unterhalten, wenn er langsam spricht und mir bei meinen Antworten hilft.

	Kann ich	Muss ich noch üben
Ich kann fragen, wie das Wetter ist, und selbst eine Frage nach dem Wetter beantworten: What's the weather like? It's rainy today.	○	○
Ich kann fragen, wie viel etwas kostet, und selbst eine Frage nach dem Preis beantworten: How much is it? The doll is £5.	○	○
Ich kann jemanden fragen, was er gerne mag, und sagen, was ich selbst mag oder nicht mag: Do you like ketchup on your chips? I like the red T-shirt. I don't like the green jacket.	○	○
Ich kann jemanden fragen, was er kann, und sagen, was ich selbst kann oder nicht kann: Can you play the guitar? I can swim. I can't sing.	○	○

Lesen: Ich kann schon einige Wörter und ein paar Sätze lesen und verstehen.

	Kann ich	Muss ich noch üben
Ich kann z. B. folgende Wörter richtig vorlesen und verstehe, was sie bedeuten:	◯	◯

Monday, banana, doll, grandma, bus, stop, go, right, left, sad, swimming

	Kann ich	Muss ich noch üben
Ich kann kurze Texte lesen und den Inhalt verstehen:	◯	◯

This is Sally.
Sally is a kangaroo.
Sally likes lollipops.

Schreiben: Ich kann schon einige Wörter schreiben und kurze Texte verfassen.

	Kann ich	Muss ich noch üben
Ich kann in einem Formular meinen Namen, mein Alter und meine Sprachen eintragen.	◯	◯
Ich kann z. B. eine Postkarte, eine kurze E-Mail oder eine Geburtstagseinladung schreiben:	◯	◯

Dear Tom,
I'm in London …

Dear Ann,
Please come to my
birthday party …

Colours	**Farben**
black	schwarz
blue	blau
brown	braun
green	grün
grey	grau
orange	orange
pink	rosa
purple	lila
red	rot
white	weiß
yellow	gelb

What colour is ...? – It's ...
Welche Farbe hat ...? – Es ist ...

Numbers	**Zahlen**
one	eins
two	zwei
three	drei
four	vier
five	fünf
six	sechs
seven	sieben
eight	acht
nine	neun
ten	zehn
eleven	elf
twelve	zwölf
thirteen	dreizehn
fourteen	vierzehn
fifteen	fünfzehn
sixteen	sechzehn
seventeen	siebzehn
eighteen	achtzehn
nineteen	neunzehn
twenty	zwanzig
thirty	dreißig
forty	vierzig
fifty	fünfzig

sixty	sechzig
seventy	siebzig
eighty	achtzig
ninety	neunzig
a/one hundred	hundert

How many ... can you see?
Wie viele ... kannst du sehen?

At school	**In der Schule**	
book	Buch	
class	Klasse	
computer	Computer	
exercise book	Heft	
(to) learn	lernen	
(to) listen	zuhören	
pen	Füller	
pencil	Bleistift	
pencil case	Federmappe	
pencil sharpener	Spitzer	
pupil	Schüler	
(to) read	lesen	
rubber	Radiergummi	
ruler	Lineal	
schoolbag	Schultasche	
(to) speak	sprechen	
stick of glue/	Klebestift	
glue stick		
teacher	Lehrer(in)	
(to) write	schreiben	

I'm in class ...
Ich bin in der ... Klasse.

Can I have your ..., please?
Darf ich bitte dein(e, en) ... haben?

Take out your ..., please.
Nehmt bitte eure ... heraus.

Me, my family and my friends — **Ich, meine Familie und meine Freunde**

aunt	Tante
brother	Bruder
cousin	Cousin/Kusine
father	Vater
grandfather/ grandpa	Großvater/ Opa
grandmother/ grandma	Großmutter/ Oma
great	großartig
mother	Mutter
(to) like	mögen
(to) love	lieben
nice	nett
old	alt
sister	Schwester
uncle	Onkel
young	jung

Hi!/Hello!
Hallo!

Goodbye!
Auf Wiedersehen!

Good morning!/Good night!
Guten Morgen!/Gute Nacht!

This is …/He is …/She is …
Das ist …/Er ist …/Sie ist …

How are you? – I'm fine, thanks.
Wie geht es dir? – Danke, gut.

What's your name? – My name is …/I'm …
Wie heißt du? – Ich heiße …

How old are you? – I'm … years old.
Wie alt bist du? – Ich bin … Jahre alt.

Homes, rooms and furniture — **Wohnungen, Zimmer und Möbel**

big	groß
castle	Schloss, Burg
farm	Bauernhof
flat	(Etagen-)Wohnung
house	Haus
igloo	Iglu
small	klein
tepee	Tipi
bathroom	Badezimmer
bedroom	Schlafzimmer
(to) close	schließen
door	Tür
kitchen	Küche
living room	Wohnzimmer
(to) open	öffnen
(to) sleep	schlafen
(to) tidy up	aufräumen
toilet	Toilette, WC
window	Fenster
bed	Bett
CD player	CD-Spieler
chair	Stuhl
cupboard	Schrank
desk	Schreibtisch
lamp	Lampe
(to) lie	liegen
shelves	Regal
(to) sit	sitzen
sofa	Sofa
table	Tisch
(to) watch TV	fernsehen

In my house there is a …
In meinem Haus gibt es ein(e,en) …

Body and face — **Körper und Gesicht**

angry	zornig
arm	Arm
(to) brush	(sich) bürsten
(to) clap	klatschen
ear	Ohr
eye	Auge
(to) feel	(sich) fühlen
finger	Finger
foot/feet	Fuß/Füße

glad	froh, fröhlich
(to) go	gehen
hair	Haar(e)
hand	Hand
happy	glücklich
(to) hear	hören
(to) hurt	wehtun
knee	Knie
leg	Bein
(to) look	(hin)sehen, (an)schauen
mouth	Mund
nose	Nase
sad	traurig
(to) run	rennen, laufen
(to) smell	riechen, duften
(to) taste	schmecken
toe	Zeh(e)
tooth/teeth	Zahn/Zähne
(to) touch	anfassen
(to) wash	(sich) waschen

How do you feel? – I feel …
Wie fühlst du dich? – Ich fühle mich/bin …

Clothes — Kleider

anorak	Anorak
boot	Stiefel
cap	Kappe
dress	Kleid
glove	Handschuh
jacket	Jacke
pullover	Pullover
(to) put on	anziehen
scarf	Schal
shirt	Hemd
shoe	Schuh
(a pair of) shorts	kurze Hose, Shorts
skirt	Rock
sock	Socke
(to) take off	ausziehen
(a pair of) trousers	Hose
T-shirt	T-Shirt
woolly hat	Wollmütze

I'm wearing a …
Ich trage ein(e,en) …

I like your …
Ich mag dein(e,en) …

Toys, sports and hobbies — Spielzeug, Sportarten und Hobbys

basketball	Basketball
bike	Fahrrad
cards	Karten
(to) do	tun, machen
drum	Trommel
football	Fußball
guitar	Gitarre
hockey	Hockey
(to) play	spielen
piano	Klavier
recorder	Blockflöte
(to) ride	reiten, fahren
(to) sing	singen
skateboard	Skateboard
(to) swim	schwimmen
teddy bear	Teddybär

What is your hobby? – My hobby is …
Was ist dein Hobby? – Mein Hobby ist …

Can you …? – Yes, I can./No, I can't.
Kannst du …? – Ja./Nein.

Food — Essen

cheese	Käse
chicken	Hühnchen
chips	Pommes (frites)
(to) cook	kochen
crisps	Chips
(to) cut	schneiden
(to) eat	essen
fish	Fisch
ham	Schinken
hamburger	Hamburger
hungry	hungrig

ketchup	Ketchup
mashed potatoes	Kartoffelbrei
pizza	Pizza
salt	Salz
sandwich	Sandwich
sausage	Wurst
soup	Suppe

What do you like? – I like …
Was magst du? – Ich mag …

What don't you like? – I don't like …
Was magst du nicht? – Ich mag … nicht.

I love to eat …
Besonders gerne esse ich …

Fruit and vegetables | **Obst und Gemüse**

apple	Apfel
banana	Banane
carrot	Karotte, Möhre
cucumber	Gurke
lemon	Zitrone
potato	Kartoffel
orange	Orange
salad	Salat
strawberry	Erdbeere
tomato	Tomate

Can I have a …, please?
Kann ich bitte eine(n) … haben?

Sweets | **Süßigkeiten**

cake	Kuchen
chocolate	Schokolade
honey	Honig
ice cream	Eiskrem
lollipop	Lutscher
sugar	Zucker

Drinks | **Getränke**

a bottle of …	eine Flasche …
coffee	Kaffee
coke	Cola
(to) drink	trinken
a glass of …	ein Glas …
lemonade	Limonade
orange juice	Orangensaft
tea	Tee
thirsty	durstig
water/	Wasser,
mineral water	Mineralwasser

What would you like to drink? –
I'd like a glass of …

Was möchtest du gerne trinken? –
Ich hätte gerne ein Glas …

Shopping | **Einkaufen**

(to) buy	kaufen
(to) fit	passen
free	kostenlos
(to) get	bekommen
(to) pay	bezahlen
(half) price	(halber) Preis
(to) sell	verkaufen
sale	(Schluss-)Verkauf
shop	Geschäft, Laden
special offer	Sonderangebot

What would you like?/Can I help you? –
I'd like …
Was hättest du gerne? –
Ich hätte gerne …

Here you are.
Hier, bitte.

How much is it? –
That's £…, please.
Das macht bitte … Pfund.

Thank you./Thanks.
Danke.

Nature	Natur
(to) climb	hochklettern
flower	Blume
garden	Garten
(to) go for a walk/	spazierengehen
(to) walk	
grass	Gras
(to) grow	wachsen
jungle	Dschungel
lake	See
moon	Mond
mountain	Berg, Gebirge
ocean	Ozean
river	Fluss
sea	Meer
(to) shine	scheinen
star	Stern
sun	Sonne
tree	Baum
(to) watch	beobachten

Wild animals	Wildtiere
bear	Bär
bird	Vogel
crocodile	Krokodil
elephant	Elefant
(to) fly	fliegen
frog	Frosch
kangaroo	Känguru
koala	Koala
monkey	Affe
snake	Schlange
wombat	Wombat
zebra	Zebra
zoo	Zoo

What's your favourite animal? –
My favourite animal is …

Was ist dein Lieblingstier? –
Mein Lieblingstier ist …

Pets	Haustiere
(to) bite	beißen
budgie	Wellensittich
cat	Katze
dog	Hund
(to) feed	füttern
fish/goldfish	Fisch/Goldfisch
guinea pig	Meerschweinchen
hamster	Hamster
mouse	Maus
rabbit	Kaninchen
(to) walk the dog	den Hund
	ausführen

What pet have you got? –
I've got a …
Was für ein Haustier hast du –
Ich habe ein(e,en) …

Farm animals	Bauernhoftiere
cow	Kuh
duck	Ente
goose	Gans
horse	Pferd
pig	Schwein
sheep	Schaf

Time, weather and seasons	Zeit, Wetter und Jahreszeiten
autumn	Herbst
birthday	Geburtstag
birthday card	Geburtstagskarte
Christmas	Weihnachten
cold	kalt
Easter	Ostern
rain	Regen
rainy	regnerisch
snow	Schnee
snowy	verschneit
spring	Frühjahr
summer	Sommer

sunny	sonnig		
warm	warm		
wind	Wind		
windy	windig		
winter	Winter		

What time is it? – It's ... o'clock.
Wie spät ist es?

When do you go to bed?
Wann gehst du ins Bett?

When is your birthday? –
My birthday is in ...
Wann hast du Geburtstag? –
Ich habe im ... Geburtstag.

What's the weather like today? –
Today it's ...
Wie ist heute das Wetter? –
Heute ist es ...

Days and months	**Tage und Monate**
Monday	Montag
Tuesday	Dienstag
Wednesday	Mittwoch
Thursday	Donnerstag
Friday	Freitag
Saturday	Samstag
Sunday	Sonntag
week	Woche
weekend	Wochenende
January	Januar
February	Februar
March	März
April	April
May	Mai
June	Juni
July	Juli
August	August
September	September
October	Oktober
November	November
December	Dezember

What day is it today? – Today is ...
Welcher Tag ist heute? – Heute ist ...

Countries	**Länder**
Australia	Australien
England	England
English	englisch
France	Frankreich
German	deutsch
Germany	Deutschland
(to) go by bus	mit dem Bus fahren
(to) go by car	mit dem Auto fahren
(to) go by plane	mit dem Flugzeug reisen
(to) go by train	mit dem Zug fahren
Great Britain	Großbritannien
Italy	Italien
(to) live	leben, wohnen
(to) meet	treffen, begegnen
Poland	Polen
Russia	Russland
Spain	Spanien
Turkey	Türkei
(the) USA	USA

Where are you from? – I'm from .../
I come from ...
Woher kommst du? – Ich komme aus ...

Where do you live? – I live in ...
Wo wohnst du? – Ich wohne in ...

Prepositions	**Präpositionen**
behind	hinter
between	zwischen
in	in
in front of	vor
next to	neben
on	auf
under	unter

Where is ...? – It's in/on/under ...
Wo ist ...? – Es ist in/auf/unter ...

Lösungen

Servus! Ich bin die Susi.

Hi! I'm Sally.

Bonjour! Je suis Robert.

1. Read the sentences. Write the correct numbers next to the pictures.

1 This is Tim. He is in class 4b.

2 This is Linda. She is in class 4b.

3 This is Susan. She is from England.

4 This is Tobi. He is from Germany.

5 This is John. He is ten years old.

6 This is Ann. She is ten years old.

5

1

4

6

3

2

2. He or she? Colour the words blue or red.

he

she

Mrs Miller

Tina

Mr Brown

dad

Simon

Jenny

John

Susan

3. What about you?

I'm = I am

Hi, I'm _____ .

I'm from _____ .

I'm _____ years old.

I'm in class _____ .

4. Tell more about yourself, your family and your friends.

_____

_____

_____

_____

Hi! How are you?

I'm fine, thanks.

I'm 10 years old. What about you?

I'm 142.

Oops!

1. Odd one out!

June, February, Monday, December

brother, teacher, sister, mother

ten, eight, one, yellow

Big Ben, Australia, Germany, Great Britain

2. Read and draw lines.

What's your name?   It's on the desk.

How old is Tim?   My name is Sally.

Where is Ann's pencil?   It's 8 o'clock.

When is your birthday?   He's 10 years old.

What time is it?   My birthday is in May.

3. Fill in: when, where, how, what.

How are you? – I'm fine, thanks.

What 's your name? – My name is Daniel.

How old are you? – I'm ten years old.

Where are you from? – I'm from England.

What is your hobby? – My hobby is playing the guitar.

When is your birthday? – My birthday is in January.

when = wann   how = wie
where = wo   what = was

4. Put the words into the correct order. Write the sentences.

old is brother how your? How **old is your brother?**

time is what it? **What time is it?**

you where live do? **Where do you live?**

is hobby what your? **What is your hobby?**

to bed when do go you? **When do you go to bed?**

Im Englischen schreibst du die meisten Wörter klein. Nur Satzanfänge, Eigennamen und einige besondere Wörter (I, Wochentage, Monate) schreibst du groß.

Unit 2: Greeting und meeting

5. Ben meets Sarah. Write the dialogue.

Grüße und stelle dich vor. Frage das Mädchen nach dem Namen.

Hello/Hi!
My name is Ben.
What's your name?

Grüße zurück und nenne deinen Namen.

Hi/Hello!
My name is Sarah.

Frage Sarah, wie es ihr geht.

How are you?

Antworte, dass es dir gut geht. Frage Ben, woher er kommt.

I'm fine, thanks.
Where are you from?

Antworte, dass du aus England kommst.

I'm from England.

Sage, dass du aus Deutschland kommst. Verabschiede dich.

I'm from Germany.
Goodbye!

Verabschiede dich.

Goodbye!

Die Sätze von Aufgabe 3 auf Seite 7 können dir helfen.

8

Kenny the koala and Walter the wombat are from Australia, too. They are my best friends.

Oh look! This is Craig. Craig isn't nice.

Craig is a crocodile and he loves to eat koalas, wombats and KANGAROOS!!

1. Read the comic.

2. What's wrong? Correct the sentences.

Sally is a cow. _Sally is a kangaroo._

Sally comes from Spain. _Sally comes from Australia._

Her best friends are Kenny the kangaroo and Walter the horse.
Her best friends are Kenny the koala and Walter the wombat.

Kenny and Walter come from Spain, too. _Kenny and Walter come from Australia, too._

Craig is Sally's friend. _Craig isn't Sally's friend._

He is nice. _He isn't nice._

He is a dog. _He is a crocodile._

He loves to eat carrots, bananas and lollipops. _He loves to eat koalas, wombats and kangaroos._

9

---

3. Match the words.

elephant   bear   cat   goldfish   sheep   crocodile
horse   rabbit   budgie   hamster   duck   goose
snake   guinea pig   zebra

wild animals
kangaroo
elephant
bear
crocodile
snake
zebra

pets
cat
dog
goldfish
rabbit
budgie
hamster
guinea pig

farm animals
cow
sheep
horse
duck
goose

10

---

4. Sally has got some pictures on her mobile phone.

Circle the correct word: is or are, isn't or aren't.

Look, this (is) / are my house.
It (isn't) / aren't very big.
Here is / (are) my friends Kenny and Walter.
Kenny and Walter isn't / (aren't) kangaroos like me.
Kenny (is) / are a koala.
Walter (is) / are a wombat.
Craig (isn't) / aren't my friend.
He (is) / are a crocodile.

In der Einzahl verwendest du im Englischen is, bei einer Verneinung isn't.
In der Mehrzahl verwendest du are, bei einer Verneinung aren't.

5. Write and talk about your pet or friend.

... is my pet/my friend.
He's/She's a ...
He's/She's ... years old.
He's/She's from ...
He's/She's big/small/ brown/nice ...

11

Lösungen

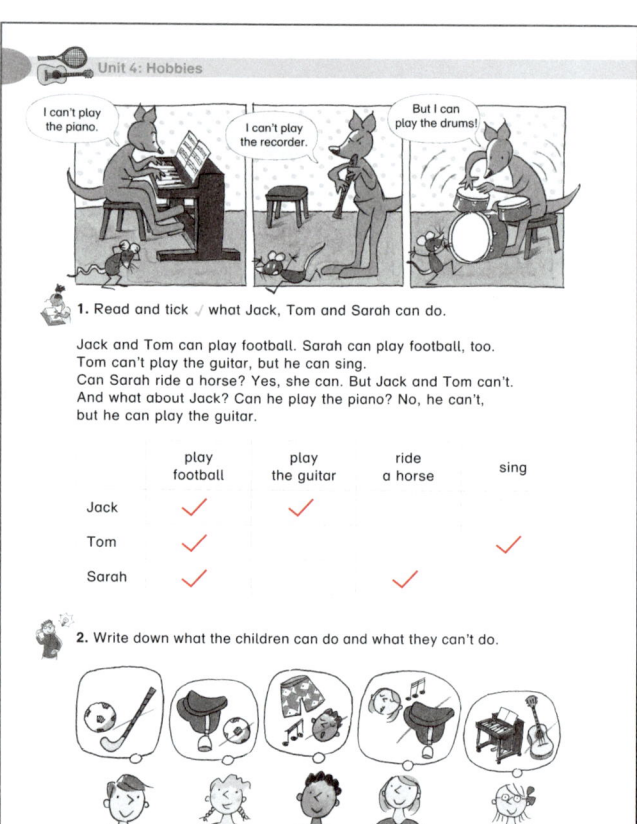

1. Read and tick ✓ what Jack, Tom and Sarah can do.

Jack and Tom can play football. Sarah can play football, too.
Tom can't play the guitar, but he can sing.
Can Sarah ride a horse? Yes, she can. But Jack and Tom can't.
And what about Jack? Can he play the piano? No, he can't,
but he can play the guitar.

	play football	play the guitar	ride a horse	sing
Jack	✓	✓		
Tom	✓			✓
Sarah	✓		✓	

2. Write down what the children can do and what they can't do.

12

Tom can play football, but he can't play hockey. _____

Tina can ride a horse, but she can't play football.

Sam can swim, but he can't sing.

Jane can sing, but she can't ride a horse.

Ann can play the piano, but she can't play the guitar.

3. Write a dialogue about Ann and Tom's hobbies.

Ann: Can you play the guitar? – Tom: Yes, I can. (weitere Beispiele)
Tom: Can you play football? – Ann: No, I can't.
Ann: Can you ride a horse? – Tom: No, I can't.
Tom: Can you play the recorder? – Ann: Yes, I can.
Ann: Can you play basketball? – Tom: Yes, I can.
Tom: Can you swim? – Ann: No, I can't.

> Wenn du etwas kannst, dann sagst du im Englischen I can (swim) ☺.
> Wenn du etwas nicht kannst, dann sagst du I can't (sing) ☹.

13

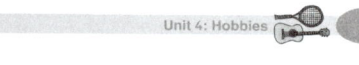

1. Where do you live? Read the sentences.
Find the correct pictures and draw lines.

I live in a castle.
I live in the ocean.
I live on a farm.
I live in an igloo.
I live in a tepee.
I live in the zoo.

2. Find 10 words in my house. Write.

kitchen, table,

garden, bed,

bathroom, sofa,

bedroom, chair,

living room, desk

14

3. Come to my castle.

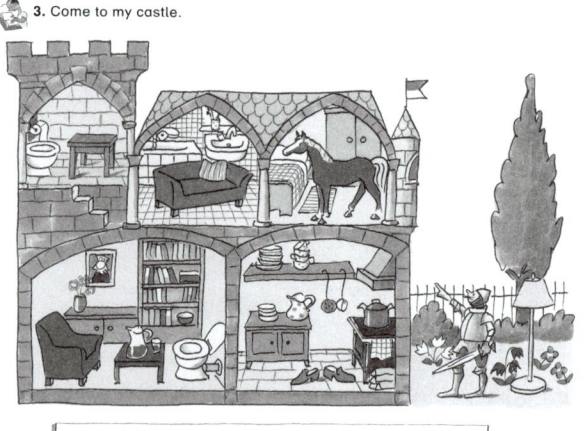

| kitchen | toilet | bathroom |
| garden | bedroom | living room |

Where is my lamp? The lamp is in the garden .

Where is my toilet? The toilet is in the living room .

Where is my horse? The horse is in the bedroom .

Where are my shoes? The shoes are in the kitchen .

Where is my sofa? The sofa is in the bathroom .

Where is my table? The table is in the toilet .

15

Unit 5: At home

The bike is in the cupboard. **The skateboard is under the bed. The hamster is on the sofa. The schoolbag is behind the shelves. The books are next to the chair. The dog is on the cupboard. The guitar is behind the door. The computer is in front of the desk.**

5. What about your room? Tell a friend.

- The books are …
- My teddy bear is …
- My schoolbag is …
- My T-shirts are …
- The bed is …
- My CD player is …

Unit 6: Going shopping

Great! A T-shirt for £2!

Mr Paper

Two for £1:

Half price:
10 pencils £3 £1.50
pencil case £12 £6
5 pens £3.60 £1.80
3 exercise books £2 £1

Special offer:
birthday card only £1.99

1. What can you buy for £1? (Beispiele)

I can buy two rulers./I can buy a rubber and a pencil sharpener.

2. What can you buy for half price?

I can buy ten pencils/a pencil case/five pens/three exercise books.

3. What did Susan buy at Mr Paper's?

	5 pens	1,80
2	**birthday cards**	3,98
6	**exercise books**	2,-
2	**rubbers/rulers/pencil sharpeners**	1,-

17

18

Unit 6: Going shopping

4. What does Sally buy at Mr Paper's?

Sally buys **two rubbers, a/one ruler, ten pencils, a/one birthday card and three exercise books.**

> Bei den meisten englischen Nomen hängst du in der Mehrzahl ein s an:
> one pencil – five pencils
> ! one sheep – six sheep, one fish – four fish, one mouse – three mice, one foot – two feet, one tooth – seven teeth !

5. Correct the mistakes.

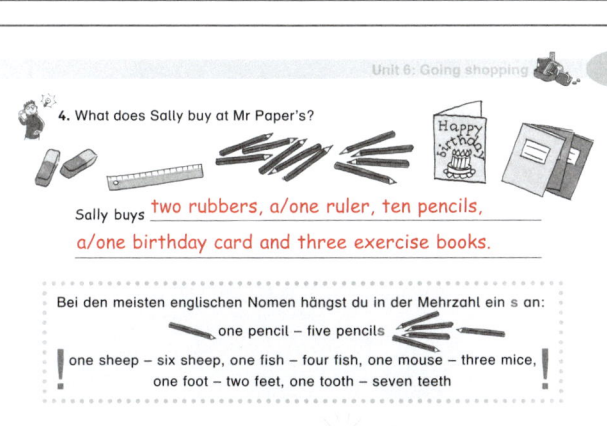

Hello
~~Good night,~~ Mr Paper.

I'd like
two ~~bananas~~, please.
rulers

Thanks.
~~Good morning,~~ Mr Paper.
Goodbye

Hello/Hi
~~Goodbye,~~ Sally.
What would you like?

are
Here you ~~swim.~~
That's £1, please.

Goodbye
~~Hello,~~ Sally.

Unit 7: Food and drinks

SALLY IN GERMANY

I'd like some chips, please.

I see! German chips are English crisps!

1. Make up the dialogue. Number the sentences in the correct order.

- (5) A glass or a bottle of mineral water?
- (3) Anything to drink?
- (7) That's four pounds, please.
- (1) Hello! Can I help you?
- (9) Thank you. Goodbye!
- (2) Hello! Yes, I'd like a hamburger.
- (8) Four pounds. Here you are.
- (4) I'd like some mineral water, please.
- (6) A bottle of mineral water.
- (10) Goodbye!

19

20

Lösungen

 **Unit 7: Food and drinks**

 3. Sally wants something to eat and drink.
Make up the dialogue.

FOOD	DRINKS
pizza £1	orange juice £1
hamburger £1	coke £1
salad with ham £1,20	lemonade £1
fish and chips £1	tea £1
cheese sandwich £1	coffee £1
chicken sandwich £1,30	water £1

 (Beispiel)

Hello! Can I help you?   Hello! I'd like fish
                              and chips.

Anything to drink?   I'd like some orange juice,
                             please.

That's two pounds,   Two pounds.
please.   Here you are.

Thank you. Goodbye!   Goodbye!

Die Sätze von Aufgabe 1
auf Seite 20 können dir helfen.
Denke auch an die Begrüßung
und Verabschiedung.

22

Tests

 Test 1: Minnie's postcard
Read and write.

Hi Grandma,

London is great.
But it's very cold and rainy.
I like the double-decker buses!
Today we are going to a museum.
We want to be back home on Sunday.
Love, Minnie

Mrs Miller
5 Main Street
Manchester
A12 3BC

Where is Minnie?
Minnie is in London.

What's the weather like?
It's very cold and rainy.

What does Minnie like?
Minnie likes the double-decker buses.

Where is Minnie going today?
Today Minnie is going to a museum.

When does Minnie want to be back home?
Minnie wants to be back home on Sunday.

23

Tests

 Test 2: Funny animals
Read and colour.

The blue mouse is under the skateboard.
The red mouse is in the cake.
The cat with green legs is on the piano.
The orange guinea pig is next to the piano.
The horse with the purple head is in the lake.
The yellow horse is riding the bike.
The green dog is playing the guitar.

 Test 3: Jumbled sentences
Put the words into the correct order.

a ruler and a book   I've got   in my schoolbag
I've got a ruler and a book in my schoolbag   .

on my desk   the pencil case   is
The pencil case is on my desk   .

is   under my folder   the book
The book is under my folder   .

24

Tests

Test 4: What can you say?
Fill in the speech bubbles.

What's ...	How much ...
How old ...	How ...

How are you   ? –
I'm fine, thanks!

How much is it   ? –
It's £5.

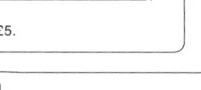
What's your favourite fruit ? –
My favourite fruit is banana.

Where are you from? –
I'm from Germany.

Can you play basketball? –
No, I can't.

How old are you   ? –
I'm 10 years old.

25